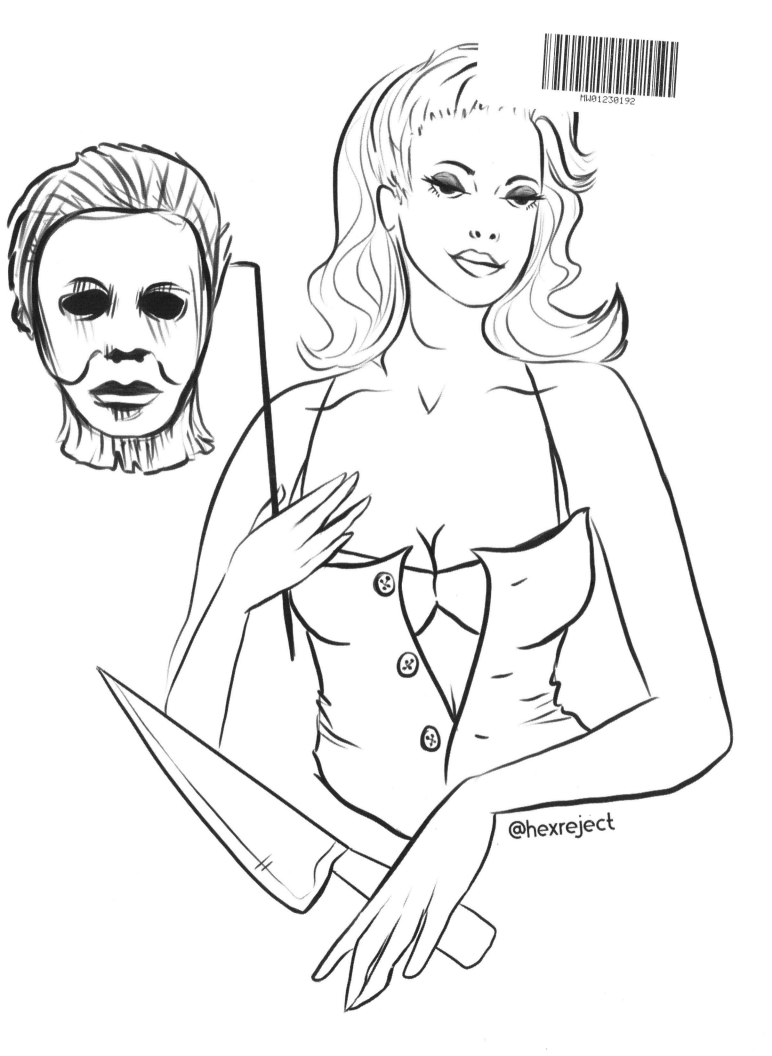

@hexreject

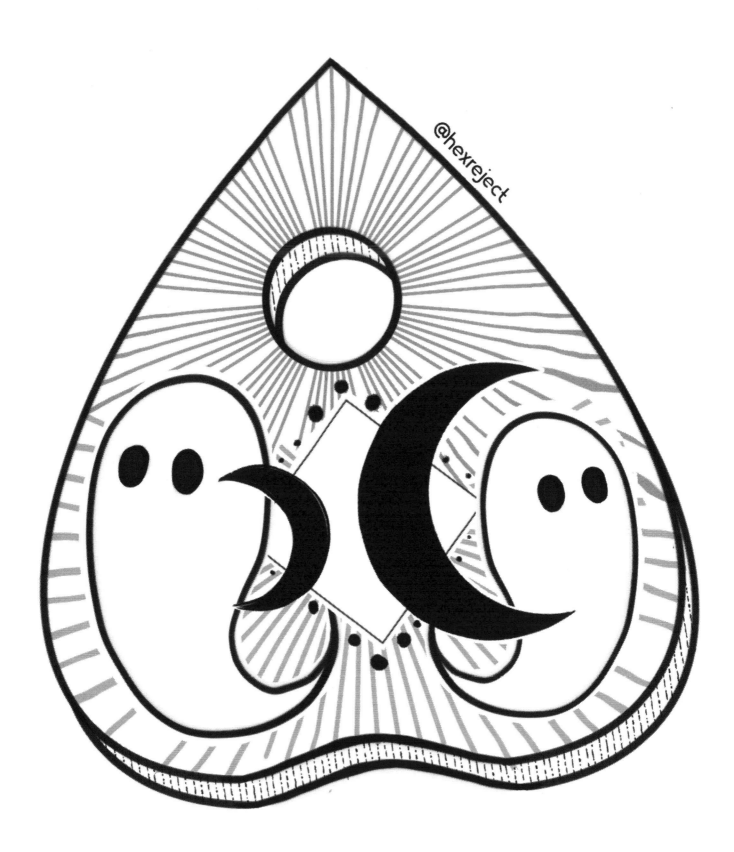

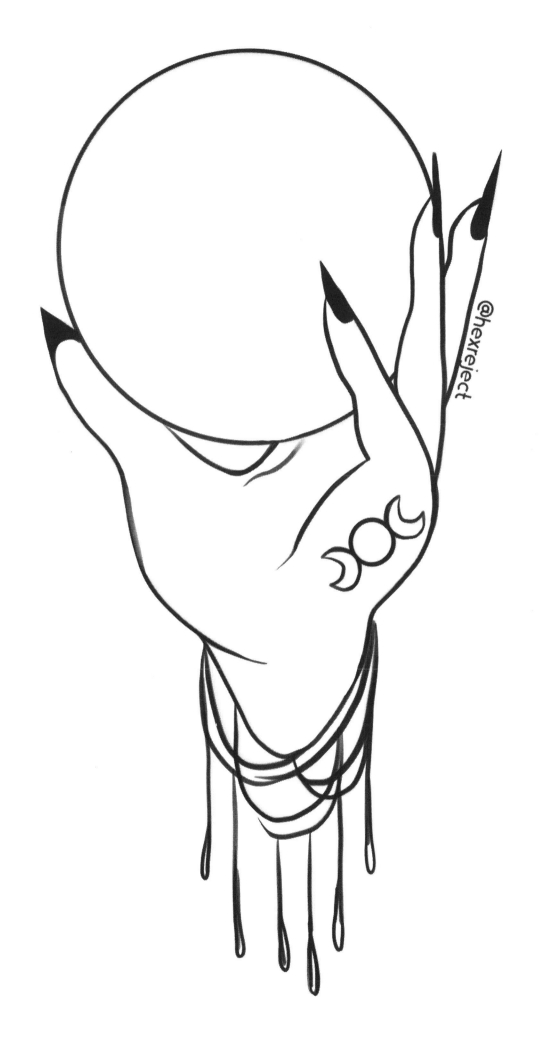

@hexreject

@hexreject

@hexreject

DEAD MEN
DON'T CATCALL

@hexreject

@hexreject

@hexreject

@hexreject

@hexreject

THE HIGH PRIESTESS

@hexreject

@hexreject

@hexreject

@hexreject

@hexreject

@hexreject

@hexreject

@hexreject

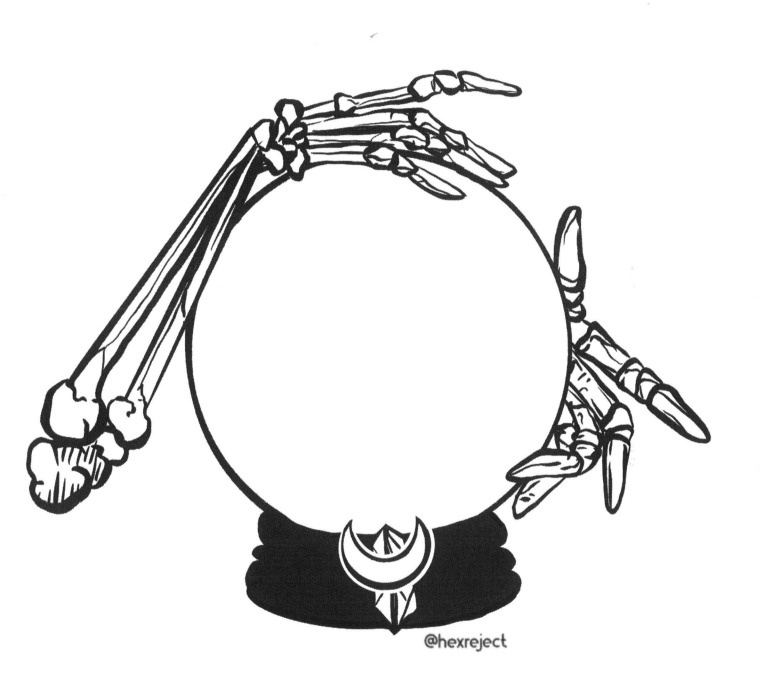

@hexreject

@hexreject

@hexreject

@hexreject

@hexreject

@hexreject

@hexreject

@hexreject

@hexreject

THE MOON

XVIIII

@hexreject

XIII

DEATH

@hexreject

THE EMPRESS

@hexreject

XV

THE DEVIL

@hexreject

XXI

THE WORLD

@hexreject

@hexreject

@hexreject

@hexreject

@hexreject

@hexreject

@hexreject

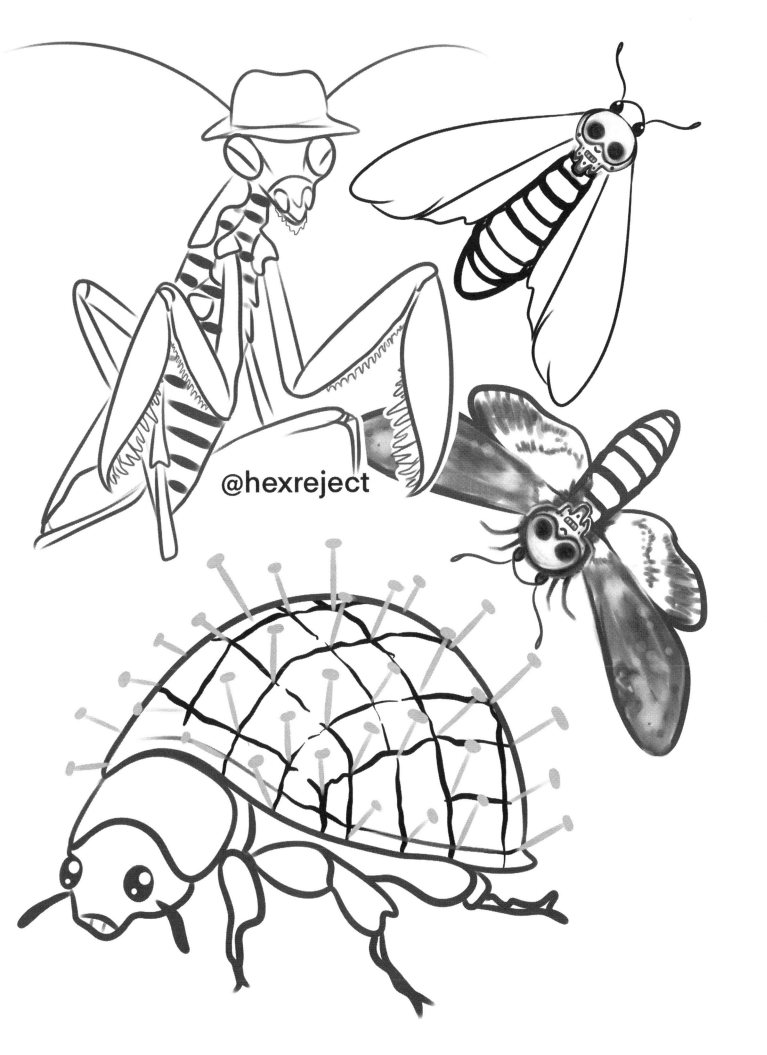

@hexreject

@hexreject

@hexreject

@hexreject

@hexreject

@hexreject

@hexreject

@hexreject

@hexreject

@hexreject

@hexreject

@hexreject

@hexreject

@hexreject

@hexreject

@hexreject

@hexreject

@hexreject

@hexreject

@hexreject

@hexreject

@hexreject

@hexreject

@hexreject

@hexreject

@hexreject

@hexreject

@hexreject

@hexreject

@hexreject

@hexreject

@hexreject

@hexreject

@hexreject

@hexreject

@hexreject

@hexreject

@hexreject

@hexreject

@hexreject

@hexreject

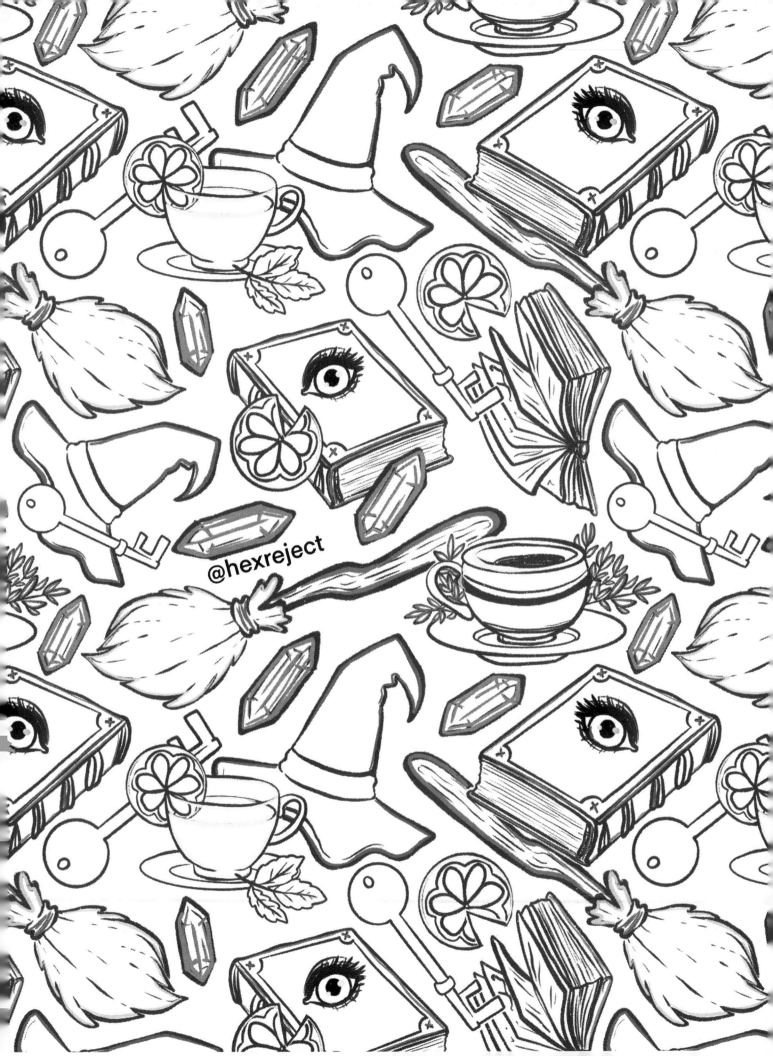

@hexreject

@hexreject

@hexreject

@hexreject

@hexreject

@hexreject

@hexreject

@hexreject

@hexreject

@hexreject

@hexreject

@hexreject

@hexreject

@hexreject

@hexreject

@hexreject

@hexreject

@hexreject

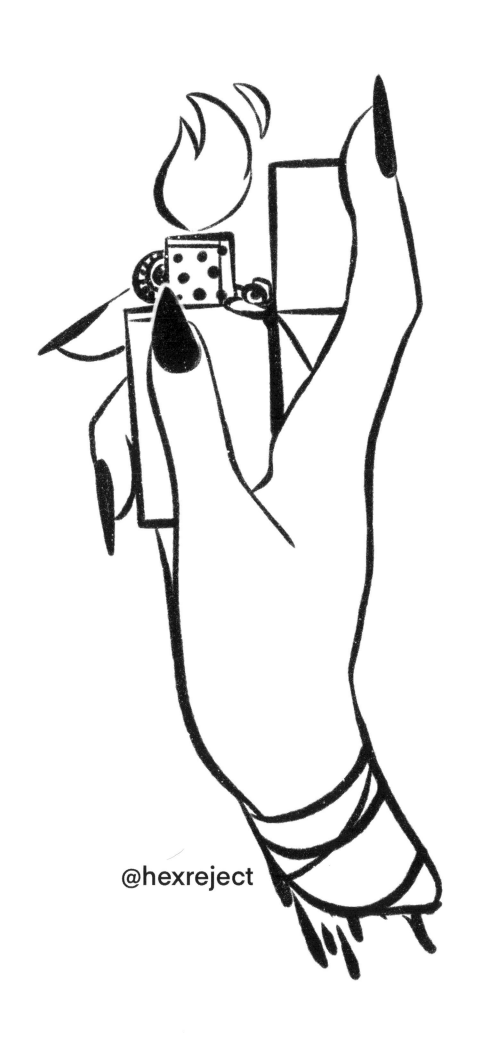

@hexreject

@hexreject

I DO WHAT I WANT

@hexreject

PLANT KILLER

@hexreject

@hexreject

@hexreject

Made in the USA
Columbia, SC
04 September 2023

22423678R00067